THE TAO OF REAGAN

**Common Sense From An
Uncommon Man**

THE TAO OF REAGAN

Common Sense From An
Uncommon Man

◆

Daniel Agatino, J.D., Ph.D.

THE TAO OF REAGAN

Common Sense From An Uncommon Man

Vinci-Agatino Enterprises LLC ™

Publisher's address:
Vinci-Agatino Enterprises, LLC
3219 Route 46 East
Parsippany, NJ 07054

ISBN: 0-9760736-5-X

Printed in the United States of America

For Jessica who is like
every color of Fall
the finest flower of Spring
a cool breeze in Summer
the first snow of Winter

Acknowledgment

Special thanks to Rob Vinci and Sharon Cece
who were vital contributors throughout the evolution
of this book.

Contents

Preface

In his lifetime Ronald Reagan was such a cheerful and invigorating presence that it was easy to forget what daunting historic tasks he set himself. He sought to mend America's wounded spirit, to restore the strength of the free world, and to free the slaves of communism. These were causes hard to accomplish and heavy with risk.

Yet they were pursued with almost a lightness of spirit. For Ronald Reagan also embodied another great cause—what Arnold Bennett once called "the great cause of cheering us all up". His politics had a freshness and optimism that won converts from every class and every nation—and ultimately from the very heart of the evil empire.

Others prophesied the decline of the West; he inspired America and its allies with renewed faith in their mission of freedom.

Others saw only limits to growth; he transformed a stagnant economy into an engine of opportunity.

Others hoped, at best, for an uneasy cohabitation with the Soviet Union; he won the Cold War—not only without firing a shot, but also by inviting enemies out of their fortress and turning them into friends.

Ronald Reagan knew his own mind. He had firm principles—and, I believe, right ones. He expounded them clearly, he acted upon them decisively.

When the world threw problems at the White House, he was not baffled, or disorientated, or overwhelmed. He knew almost instinctively what to do.

When his aides were preparing option papers for his decision, they were able to cut out entire rafts of proposals that they knew 'the Old Man' would never wear.

When his allies came under Soviet or domestic pressure, they could look confidently to Washington for firm leadership.

And when his enemies tested American resolve, they soon discovered that his resolve was firm and unyielding.

Yet his ideas, though clear, were never simplistic. He saw the many sides of truth.

Ronald Reagan carried the American people with him in his great endeavors because there was perfect sympathy between them. He and they loved America and what it stands for—freedom and opportunity for ordinary people.

As an actor in Hollywood's golden age, he helped to make the American dream live for millions all over the globe. His own life was a fulfillment of that dream. He never succumbed to the embarrassment some people feel about an honest expression of love of country.

He was able to say 'God Bless America' with equal fervor in public and in private. And so he was able to call confidently upon his fellow-countrymen to make sacrifices for America—and to make sacrifices for those who looked to America for hope and rescue.

. . . (W)e have one beacon to guide us that Ronald Reagan never had. We have his example. Let us give thanks today for a life that achieved so much for all of God's children.

—*Excerpts quoted from Margaret Thatcher's eulogy for President Reagan, June 11, 2004.*

Introduction

What is the Tao (pronounced *Dow*)? The word describes an ancient Chinese concept that can be translated as "way" but in reality the Tao is much more profound. C.S. Lewis defined it this way:

> It is the doctrine of objective value, the belief
> that certain attitudes are really true, and others
> are really false...This thing which I have called
> for convenience the Tao, and which others may
> call Natural Law, or Traditional Morality...is
> not one among a series of possible systems of
> value. It is the sole source of all value judgments.
>
> —C.S. Lewis, The Abolition of Man

Ronald Reagan understood the Tao, although he likely would have used a more western term such as "Natural Law." He had a firm grasp on objective morality and based his entire political philosophy on the belief that our world is governed by certain unalterable truths.

The most profound of these truths have been memorialized in The Declaration of Independence: *"We hold these truths to be self-evident, that all men are created equal, that they are endowed by their Creator with certain unalienable Rights, that among these are Life, Liberty and the pursuit of Happiness."* Reagan lived by these words, recognizing what so many others missed, that along with these awesome rights came equally extraordinary responsibilities.

Ronald Reagan was an unapologetic conservative who allowed himself to be underestimated by his opponent because it allowed him greater freedom to pursue his lofty goals. During his first term as President the U.S. economy was in shambles, Soviet leaders were determined to expand their Evil Empire, and the American people were gloomy. A number of economists, Washington-insiders and media elite saw little hope for a brighter future. They argued that America's future would be a stable diet of more of the same bad news. Reagan began proposing solutions to America's many problems but immediately met with scorn and ridicule. Economists labeled his budget proposals "voodoo economics"; career diplomats were horrified at Reagan's frank assessment of the Soviet Union as an Evil Empire and they labeled him a simpleton. But Reagan would have none of this defeatist attitude. He instinctively knew that Americans—the entire world really—longed to follow a strong, capable, optimistic leader. He was a political alchemist who wanted to transform lead-laden problems into golden opportunities. So he bypassed so-called experts and brought his case directly to the American people.

Americans responded and the President's popularity soared. Reagan made people feel good about themselves and their country. In his eight years as Commander-in-chief the economy boomed, patriotism soared and the Soviet Union collapsed. His policies helped to liberate citizens of oppressed regimes across the globe and served to relieve Americans of the unjust burdens of over-regulation and government intrusion. His strong belief in a free market, a limited government and a self-reliant citizenry defined him as a capitalist in the purest sense of the word. He trusted in America's ingenuity and entrepreneurial spirit, and he was not disappointed.

Reagan may have brought out the finest in average Americans but his successes and gentle demeanor surely brought out the worst in his critics. Many of his detractors who once claimed that America would never again be great were stupefied by Reagan's successes and reverted to arguing that all of these incredible achievements were somehow inevitable. What they failed to realize is that a country's history, much like an individual's life, does not follow an inevitable course but must be directed by strong-willed, principled leadership. In spite of the malice directed against him by some of his ideological opponents, Reagan did not return their hatred. He was a gentleman who forever dispelled the myth that conservatives are cold-hearted, stuffy elitists with no connections with average Americans. On the contrary, he proved that conservatives *are* average Americans.

Ronald Reagan left the White House in 1988 but his legacy will endure for decades, perhaps centuries. He was called the Great Communicator because of his mastery of metaphor and his warmth and sense of humor. Reagan self-proclaimed: "Whatever else history may say about me when I'm gone, I hope it will record that I appealed to your best hopes, not your worst fears." Certainly there is no better description of the Tao than this.

1

America

Freedom

"Freedom is the right to question and change the established way of doing things. It is the continuous revolution of the marketplace. It is the understanding that allows us to recognize shortcomings and seek solutions."

—*Address at Moscow State University, May 31, 1988.*

The Presidency

"When people tell me I became president on January 20, 1981, I feel I have to correct them. You don't become president of the United States. You are given temporary custody of an institution called the presidency, which belongs to our people."

—*Address to the Republican National Convention, August 15, 1988.*

Government Power

"We are a nation that has a government—not the other way around. And this makes us special among the nations of the Earth. Our government has no power except that granted it by the people. It is time to check and reverse the growth of government which shows signs of having grown beyond the consent of the governed."

—*Inaugural Address, January 20, 1981.*

Hope

"In this springtime of hope, some lights seem eternal; America's is."

—*Republican National Committee speech, August 23, 1984.*

Special Interest Groups

"We hear much of special interest groups. Our concern must be for a special interest group that has been too long neglected. It knows no sectional boundaries or ethnic and racial divisions, and it crosses political party lines. It is made up of men and women who raise our food, patrol our streets, man our mines and our factories, teach our children, keep our homes, and heal us when we are sick—professionals, industrialists, shopkeepers, clerks, cabbies, and truck drivers. They are, in short, 'We the people,' this breed called Americans."

—*Inaugural address, January 20, 1981.*

Self-government

"This is the issue of this election: whether we believe in our capacity for self-government or whether we abandon the American Revolution and confess that a little intellectual elite in a far-distant capital can plan our lives for us better than we can plan for ourselves."

—Nationally televised speech for presidential candidate Barry Goldwater, October 27, 1964.

Levels of Government

"All of us need to be reminded that the federal government did not create the states, the states created the federal government. . . . Steps will be taken aimed a restoring the balance between the various levels of government."

—*Inaugural address, January 20, 1981.*

American Influence

"It was leadership here at home that gave us strong American influence abroad, and the collapse of imperial Communism. Great nations have responsibilities to lead, and we should always be cautious of those who would lower our profile, because they might just wind up lowering our flag."

—*Republican National Committee Annual Gala, February 3, 1994.*

Communism

"The years ahead will be great ones for our country, for the cause of freedom and the spread of civilization. The West will not contain Communism, it will transcend Communism. We will not bother to denounce it, we'll dismiss it as a sad, bizarre chapter in human history whose last pages are even now being written."

—*Speech at Notre Dame University, May 17, 1981.*

This Blessed Land

"I've always believed that this blessed land was set apart in a special way, that some divine plan placed this great continent here between the two oceans to be found by people from every corner of the Earth—people who had a special love for freedom and the courage to uproot themselves, leave their homeland and friends to come to a strange land. And, when coming here, they created something new in all the history of mankind—a country where man is not beholden to government, government is beholden to man."

—Address given at The National Religious Broadcasters convention, January 31, 1983.

America's Effort

"The crisis we are facing today... does require, however, our best effort, and our willingness to believe in ourselves, and to believe in our capacity to perform great deeds; to believe that together, with God's help, we can and will resolve the problems which now confront us. And after all, why shouldn't we believe that? We are Americans. God bless you, and thank you."

—*First Inaugural Address, January 20, 1981.*

Protecting Freedom

Freedom is never more than one generation away from extinction. We didn't pass it to our children in the bloodstream. It must be fought for, protected, and handed on for them to do the same, or one day we will spend our sunset years telling our children and our children's children what it was once like in the United States where men were free.

—*Attributed to President Reagan.*

Dream of America

"The explicit promise in the Declaration that we're endowed by our Creator with certain inalienable rights was meant for all of us. It wasn't meant to be limited or perverted by special privilege or by double standards...Trusting in God and helping one another, we can and will preserve the dream of America, the last best hope of man on earth."

—*Speech given at the Annual Meeting of the American Bar Association, Atlanta, Georgia, August 1, 1983.*

America's Cause

"So, you can see why, to me, the story of these last eight years and this presidency goes far beyond any personal concerns. It is a continuation, really, of a far larger story, a story of a people and a cause. A cause that, from our earliest beginnings, has defined us as a nation and given purpose to our national existence. The hope of human freedom, the quest for it, the achievement of it, is the American saga."

—*Final radio address as president, January 14, 1989.*

2
The Economy

National Debt

"An almost unbroken 50 years of deficit spending has finally brought us to a time of reckoning. We have come to a turning point, a moment for hard decisions. I have asked the Cabinet and my staff a question, and now I put the same question to all of you: If not us, who? And if not now, when? It must be done by all of us going forward with a program aimed at reaching a balanced budget. We can then begin reducing the national debt."

—*Second Inaugural Address, January 21, 1985.*

Prosperity

"We're the party that wants to see an America in which people can still get rich."

—*Said at the Republican Congressional Dinner, Washington, D.C., May 4, 1982.*

Deficit

"For decades, we have piled deficit upon deficit, mortgaging our future and our children's future for the temporary convenience of the present. To continue this long trend is to guarantee tremendous social, cultural, political, and economic upheavals. You and I, as individuals, can, by borrowing, live beyond our means, but for only a limited period of time. Why, then, should we think that collectively, as a nation, we are not bound by that same limitation?"

—*First Inaugural Address, January 20, 1981.*

Spending

"We don't have a trillion-dollar debt because we haven't taxed enough; we have a trillion-dollar debt because we spend too much."

—*Address to National Association of Realtors, March 28, 1982.*

Government Control

"The Founding Fathers knew a government can't control the economy without controlling people. And they knew when a government sets out to do that, it must use force and coercion to achieve its purpose."

—*Nationally televised speech for presidential candidate Barry Goldwater, October 27, 1964.*

Birthright

"We believed then and now: There are no limits to growth and human progress, when men and women are free to follow their dreams. And we were right to believe that. Tax rates have been reduced, inflation cut dramatically and more people are employed than ever before in our history. We are creating a nation once again vibrant, robust, and alive. There are many mountains yet to climb. We will not rest until every American enjoys the fullness of freedom, dignity, and opportunity as our birthright. It is our birthright as citizens of this great republic."

—*Second Inaugural Address, January 21, 1985.*

Federal Budget

"The size of the federal budget is not an appropriate barometer of social conscience or charitable concern."

—Address to the National Alliance of Business, October 5, 1981.

The Objective

"This Administration's objective will be a healthy, vigorous, growing economy."

—*First Inaugural Address, January 20, 1981.*

Welfare

"Welfare's purpose should be to eliminate, as far as possible, the need for its own existence."

—*Los Angeles Times, January 7, 1970.*

People's Business

"Government is the people's business and every man, woman and child becomes a shareholder with the first penny of tax paid."

—*Address to the New York City Partnership Association, January 14, 1982.*

Human Capacity

"There are no such things as limits to growth, because there are no limits on the human capacity for intelligence, imagination and wonder."

—*Speech given to the University of South Carolina, Columbia, September 20, 1983.*

The Problem

"Government is not the solution, it's the problem."

—Inaugural address, January 20, 1981.

Tax Code

"The current tax code is a daily mugging."

—*Labor Day address, Independence Missouri, September 2, 1985.*

3
God

Divine Guidance

"May all of you as Americans never forget your heroic origins, never fail to seek divine guidance and never lose your natural, God-given optimism."

—*Speech to Republican National Convention, August 17, 1992.*

Religious Freedom

"Throughout our history, Americans have put their faith in God, and no one can doubt that we have been blessed for it. The earliest settlers of this land came in search of religious freedom. Landing on a desolate shoreline, they established a spiritual foundation that has served us ever since. It was the hard work of our people, the freedom they enjoyed and their faith in God that built this country and made it the envy of the world. In all of our great cities and towns evidence of the faith of our people is found: Houses of worship of every denomination are among the oldest structures."

—*Proclamation issued on National Day of Prayer, March 19, 1981.*

Legacy

"Let us resolve tonight that young Americans will always ... find there a city of hope in a country that is free.... And let us resolve they will say of our day and our generation, we did keep the faith with our God, that we did act worthy of ourselves, that we did protect and pass on lovingly that shining city on a hill."

—*Election eve speech, November 3, 1980.*

Faith of the Free

"Government growing beyond our consent had become a lumbering giant, slamming shut the gates of opportunity, threatening to crush the very roots of our freedom. What brought America back? The American people brought us back—with quiet courage and common sense; with undying faith that in this nation under God the future will be ours, for the future belongs to the free."

—*State of the Union Address, February 4, 1986.*

Liberation

"The men of Normandy had faith that what they were doing was right, faith that they fought for all humanity, faith that a just God would grant them mercy on this beachhead or the next. It was the deep knowledge—and pray God we have not lost it—that there is a profound moral difference between the use of force for liberation and the use of force for conquest."

—*Speech commemorating D-day invasion given in Normandy, France, June 6, 1984.*

Remembering

"We will never forget them, nor the last time we saw them—this morning, as they prepared for their journey, and waved good-bye, and 'slipped the surly bonds of earth' to 'touch the face of God.'"

—*Speech on The Challenger Disaster from the Oval Office of the White House, January 28, 1986.*

Spiritual Faith

"At every crucial turning point in our history Americans have faced and overcome great odds, strengthened by spiritual faith. The Plymouth settlers triumphed over hunger, disease, and a cruel Northern wilderness because, in the words of William Bradford, 'They knew they were Pilgrims, so they committed themselves to the will of God and resolved to proceed.' George Washington knelt in prayer at Valley Forge and in the darkest days of our struggle for independence said that 'the fate of unborn millions will now depend, under God, on the courage and conduct of this army.' Thomas Jefferson, perhaps the wisest of our founding fathers, had no doubt about the source from which our cause was derived. 'The God who gave us life,' he declared, 'gave us liberty.' And nearly a century later, in the midst of a tragic and at times seemingly hopeless Civil War, Abraham Lincoln vowed that 'this nation, under God, shall have a new birth of freedom.'"

—*Delivered during a radio broadcast to the nation, September 18, 1982.*

The Bible

"We're blessed to have its words of strength, comfort, and truth. I'm accused of being simplistic at times with some of the problems that confront us. But I've often wondered: Within the covers of that single Book are all the answers to all the problems that face us today, if we'd only look there. 'The grass withereth, the flower fadeth, but the word of our God shall stand forever.' I hope Americans will read and study the Bible in 1983. It's my firm belief that the enduring values, as I say, presented in its pages have a great meaning for each of us and for our nation. The Bible can touch our hearts, order our minds, refresh our souls."

—*Address given at The National Religious Broadcasters convention, January 31, 1983.*

The Classroom

"If we get the federal government out of the classroom, maybe we'll get God back in."

—*Washingtonian Magazine, July 1976.*

Eternal Optimism

"In closing let me thank you, the American people, for giving me the great honor of allowing me to serve as your president. When the Lord calls me home, whenever that may be, I will leave with the greatest love for this country of ours and eternal optimism for its future. I now begin the journey that will lead me into the sunset of my life. I know that for America there will always be a bright dawn ahead."

—*Speech announcing he had Alzheimer's disease, November 5, 1994.*

Religious Broadcasting

"As far as I'm concerned, the growth of religious broadcasting is one of the most heartening signs in America today."

—*Address given at The National Religious Broadcasters convention, January 31, 1983.*

Prince of Peace

"Think of it: the most awesome military machine in history, but it is no match for that one, single man, hero, strong yet tender, Prince of Peace. His name alone, Jesus, can lift our hearts, soothe our sorrows, heal our wounds, and drive away our fears. He gave us love and forgiveness. He taught us truth and left us hope. In the Book of John is the promise that we all go by—tells us that 'For God so loved the world that He gave His only begotten Son, that whosoever believeth in Him should not perish, but have everlasting life.'"

—*Address given at The National Religious Broadcasters convention, January 31, 1983.*

In God We Trust

"Our Nation's motto—'In God We Trust'—was not chosen lightly. It reflects a basic recognition that there is a divine authority in the universe to which this nation owes homage."

—*National Day of Prayer Proclamation, March 19, 1981.*

Religious Values

"To those who cite the First Amendment as reason for excluding God from more and more of our institutions and every-day life, may I just say: The First Amendment of the Constitution was not written to protect the people of this country from religious values; it was written to protect religious values from government tyranny."

—*Speech given to the Alabama State Legislature, March 15, 1982.*

America's Prayer

"Through the storms of Revolution, Civil War, and the great World Wars, as well as during the times of disillusionment and disarray, the nation has turned to God in prayer for deliverance. We thank Him for answering our call, for, surely, He has. As a nation, we have been richly blessed with His love and generosity."

—*Address given proclaiming a National Day of Prayer, February 12, 1982.*

4
Pop Culture

Baseball

"This is really more fun than being President. I really do love baseball and I wish we could do this on the lawn every day."

—*Old-Timers Game, 1983.*

Self-Delusion

"If history teaches anything, it teaches self-delusion in the face of unpleasant facts is folly."

—*Speech to the House of Commons, June 8, 1982.*

Duty

"They say the world has become too complex for simple answers. They are wrong. There are no easy answers, but there are simple answers. We must have the courage to do what we know is morally right. Winston Churchill said that "the destiny of man is not measured by material computation. When great forces are on the move in the world, we learn we are spirits—not animals." And he said, "There is something going on in time and space, and beyond time and space, which, whether we like it or not, spells duty."

—*Nationally televised speech for presidential candidate Barry Goldwater, October 27, 1964.*

Human Life

"I have been one who believes that abortion is the taking of a human life... The fact that they could not resolve the issue of when life begins was a finding in and of itself. If we don't know, then shouldn't we morally opt on the side of life? If you came upon an immobile body and you yourself could not determine whether it was dead or alive, I think that you would decide to consider it alive until somebody could prove it was dead. You wouldn't get a shovel and start covering it up. And I think we should do the same thing with regard to abortion."

—*News Conference, January 19, 1982,*

Past and Future

"Now, as most of you know, I'm not one for looking back. I figure there will be plenty of time for that when I get old. But rather, what I take from the past is inspiration for the future, and what we accomplished during our years at the White House must never be lost amid the rhetoric of political revisionists."

—*Republican National Committee Annual Gala, February 3, 1994.*

Microphones

"I am paying for this microphone, Mr. Breen."

—Said at a debate funded by Reagan after someone attempted to shut off his microphone, New Hampshire Primaries, 1980.

Inhaling

"When you see all that rhetorical smoke billowing up from the Democrats, well ladies and gentleman, I'd follow the example of their nominee; don't inhale."

—Said in reference to Bill Clinton, who admitted to smoking marijuana but not inhaling, Republican National Convention, 1992.

The Reagan Revolution

"We've done our part. And as I walk off into the city streets, a final word to the men and women of the Reagan revolution, the men and women across America who for 8 years did the work that brought America back. My friends: We did it. We weren't just marking time. We made a difference. We made the city stronger, we made the city freer, and we left her in good hands. All in all, not bad, not bad at all."

—*Farewell Address to the nation, January 20th, 1989.*

History and War

"History teaches that wars begin when govern-ments believe the price of aggression is cheap."

—*Address to the nation, January 16, 1984.*

Community Issues

"Are you willing to spend time studying the issues, making yourself aware, and then conveying that information to family and friends? Will you resist the temptation to get a government handout for your community? Realize that the doctor's fight against socialized medicine is your fight. We can't socialize the doctors without socializing the patients. Recognize that government invasion of public power is eventually an assault upon your own business. If some among you fear taking a stand because you are afraid of reprisals from customers, clients, or even government, recognize that you are just feeding the crocodile hoping he'll eat you last."

—*Nationally televised speech for presidential candidate Barry Goldwater, October 27, 1964.*

Space Program

"We've grown used to wonders in this century. It's hard to dazzle us. But for twenty-five years the United States space program has been doing just that. We've grown used to the idea of space, and perhaps we forget that we've only just begun. We're still pioneers."

—*Speech on The Challenger Disaster from the Oval Office of the White House, January 28, 1986.*

5
Humor

April 15th

"Republicans believe every day is the Fourth of July, but Democrats believe every day is April 15."

—*The New York Times, October 10, 1984.*

Tax Increases

"I have only one thing to say to the tax increasers: Go ahead, make my day."

—Said in a speech promising to veto legislation proposing a tax hike, March 13, 1985.

Economic Cycles

"Recession is when your neighbor loses his job. Depression is when you lose yours. And recovery is when Jimmy Carter loses his."

—Spoken during a campaign against Jimmy Carter, recalled at a dedication of Carter Presidential Center in Atlanta, October 2, 1986.

.

Photography

"Just remember my best side is my right side—
my far right side."

—*To White House News Photographers Association, May 18, 1983.*

Government Assistance

"The nine most terrifying words in the English language are, 'I'm from the government and I'm here to help.'"

—*Discussing aid to farmers at a Chicago press conference, August 12, 1986.*

Anti-Communism

"How do you tell a Communist? Well, it's someone who reads Marx and Lenin. And how do
you tell an anti-Communist? It's someone who
understands Marx and Lenin."

—*Remarks made in Arlington, Virginia, September 25, 1987.*

Timing

"Honey, I forgot to duck."

—Speaking to Nancy Reagan, his wife, while recovering from a gun-shot wound inflicted by John Hinckley on March 30, 1981.

Partisanship

"I hope you're all Republicans."

—Speaking to surgeons before he was to undergo an operation for his gunshot wound, March 30, 1981.

Age

"I will not make age an issue in this campaign. I am not going to exploit for political purposes my opponent's youth and inexperience."

—Spoken by 73-year-old Reagan to 56-year-old Walter Mondale, October 21, 1984.

Soviet Union

"My fellow Americans, I'm pleased to tell you today that I've signed legislation that will outlaw Russia forever. We begin bombing in five minutes."

—*Joking while testing a microphone for Saturday broadcast, August 11, 1984.*

Cabinet Meetings

"I have left orders to be awakened at any time in case of national emergency, even if I'm in a cabinet meeting."

—*Attributed to President Reagan.*

Birthdays

"I did turn 75 today—but remember, that's only 24 Celsius."

—*Commenting on his birthday, February 6, 1986.*

Work

"It's true hard work never killed anybody, but I figure, why take the chance?"

—*Favorite quip often used by President Reagan.*

Blame

Reporter Sam Donaldson: "Mr. President, in talking about the continuing recession tonight, you have blamed the mistakes of the past and you've blamed Congress. Does any of the blame belong to you?" President Reagan: "Yes, because for many years I was a Democrat."

—*Press Conference, 1982.*

The Economy

"Government's view of the economy could be summed up in a few short phrases: If it moves, tax it. If it keeps moving, regulate it. And if it stops moving, subsidize it."

—*Remarks to the White House Conference on Small Business, August 15, 1986.*

Government

"Government is like a baby. An alimentary canal with a big appetite at one end and no sense of responsibility at the other."

—Said while campaigning for Governor of California in 1965.

Politics

"Politics is just like show business. You have a hell of an opening, you coast for awhile, you have a hell of a closing."

—*Attributed to President Reagan.*

Writing

"Politics is not a bad profession. If you succeed there are many rewards, if you disgrace yourself you can always write a book."

—*Attributed to President Reagan.*

Actors

"What makes him think a middle-aged actor, who's played with a chimp, could have a future in politics?"

—*Commenting on Clint Eastwood's candidacy to be Mayor of Carmel, California.*

Eternal life

"I've always stated that the nearest thing to eternal life we'll ever see on this earth is a government program."

—*Remark made April 1986.*

Oldest Profession

"Politics is supposed to be the second oldest profession. I have come to realize that it bears a very close resemblance to the first."

—*Remark made March 3, 1978.*

Character

"You can tell a lot about a fella's character by whether he picks out all of one color or just grabs a handful."

—Referring to Reagan's jar of jelly beans kept nearby during important meetings.

6

Politics

Congress

"Cures were developed for which there were no known diseases."

—*Remarks made about Congress and their budget, 1981.*

Freedom vs. Security

"You and I are told we must choose between a left or right, but I suggest there is no such thing as a left or right. There is only an up or down. Up to man's age-old dream—the maximum of individual freedom consistent with order—or down to the ant heap of totalitarianism. Regardless of their sincerity, their humanitarian motives, those who would sacrifice freedom for security have embarked on this downward path. Plutarch warned, "The real destroyer of the liberties of the people is he who spreads among them bounties, donations and benefits."

—*Nationally televised speech for presidential candidate Barry Goldwater, October 27, 1964.*

Liberalism

"Although the political landscape has changed, the bold ideas of the 1980's are alive and well... and as a result, it seems that our opponents have finally realized how unpopular liberalism really is. So now they're trying to dress their liberal agenda in a conservative overcoat."

—*Republican Annual Gala, February 3, 1994.*

Goal of Government

"It is not my intention to do away with government. It is rather to make it work—work with us, not over us; stand by our side, not ride on our back. Government can and must provide opportunity, not smother it; foster productivity, not stifle it."

—*First Inaugural Address, January 20, 1981.*

False Statements

"However, our task is far from over. Our friends in the other party will never forgive us for our success, and are doing everything in their power to rewrite history. Listening to the liberals, you'd think that the 1980's were the worst period since the Great Depression, filled with suffering and despair. I don't know about you, but I'm getting awfully tired of the whining voices from the White House these days. They're claiming there was a decade of greed and neglect, but you and I know better than that. We were there."

—*Republican Annual Gala, February 3, 1994.*

Private Sector

"Public servants say, always with the best of intentions, 'What greater service we could render if only we had a little more money and a little more power.' But the truth is that outside of its legitimate function, government does nothing as well or as economically as the private sector."

—*Nationally televised speech for presidential candidate Barry Goldwater, October 27, 1964.*

Imitation

"After watching the State of the Union address the other night, I'm reminded of the old adage that imitation is the sincerest form of flattery. Only in this case, it's not flattery, but grand larceny: the intellectual theft of ideas that you and I recognize as our own. Speech delivery counts for little on the world stage unless you have convictions, and, yes, the vision to see beyond the front row seats."

—*Republican National Committee Annual Gala, February 3, 1994.*

Humanitarian Efforts

"Yet any time you and I question the schemes of the do-gooders, we're denounced as being opposed to their humanitarian goals. It seems impossible to legitimately debate their solutions with the assumption that all of us share the desire to help the less fortunate."

—*Nationally televised speech for presidential candidate Barry Goldwater, October 27, 1964.*

Courage

"Above all, we must realize that no arsenal, or no weapon in the arsenals of the world, is so formidable as the will and moral courage of free men and women. It is a weapon our adversaries in today's world do not have."

—*First Inaugural Address, January 20, 1981.*

Tyranny

"It is the Soviet Union that runs against the tide of history. . . . [It is] the march of freedom and democracy which will leave Marxism—Leninism on the ash heap of history as it has left other tyrannies which stifle the freedom and muzzle the self-expression of the people."

—*Speech to Britain's Parliament, June 8, 1982.*

Delegating

"Surround yourself with the best people you can find, delegate authority, and don't interfere."

—*Fortune Magazine, September 15, 1986.*

Bureaucracy

"We are for aiding our allies by sharing our material blessings with nations which share our fundamental beliefs, but we are against doling out money government to government, creating bureaucracy, if not socialism, all over the world."

—*Nationally televised speech for presidential candidate Barry Goldwater, October 27, 1964.*

7
Miscellaneous

Loyalty

"We have to move ahead, but we are not going to leave anyone behind."

—*Republican National Convention, July 1980.*

Guns

"It's just plain common sense that there be a waiting period to allow local law enforcement officials to conduct background checks on those who wish to buy a handgun."

—*Endorsing the Brady handgun control bill, March 1991.*

First Amendment

"Well, it might interest those critics to know
that none other than the Father of our Country,
George Washington, kissed the Bible at his inau-
guration. And he also said words to the effect
that there could be no real morality in a society
without religion.
. . . So, when I hear the first amendment used as
a reason to keep the traditional moral values
away from policymaking, I'm shocked. The first
amendment was not written to protect people
and their laws from religious values; it was written to protect those values from government
tyranny."

—*Address given at The National Religious Broadcasters convention,
January 31, 1983.*

Nuclear Arms

"A (nuclear weapons) freeze now would be a very dangerous fraud, for that is merely the illusion of peace. The reality is that we must find peace through strength. . . . I urge you to beware the temptation of pride, the temptation of blithely declaring yourselves above it all and label both sides equally at fault, to ignore the facts of history and the aggressive impulses of an evil empire, to simply call the arms race a giant misunderstanding and thereby remove yourself from the struggle between right and wrong and good and evil."

—*Speech to the National Association of Evangelicals, March 1983.*

Berlin

"If you seek peace, if you seek prosperity for the Soviet Union and Eastern Europe, if you seek liberalization: Come here, to this gate. Mr. Gorbachev, open this gate. Mr. Gorbachev, tear down this wall."

—*Speech at the Berlin Wall, June 12, 1987.*

Unity

"Your dreams, your hopes, your goals are going to be the dreams, the hopes, and the goals of this administration, so help me God."

—*First Inaugural address, January 20, 1981.*

Love

"If I ache, it's because we are apart and yet that can't be because you are inside and a part of me, so we really aren't apart at all. Yet I ache but wouldn't be without the ache, because that would mean being without you and that I can't be because I love you."

—*1963 love letter written to his wife, Nancy Reagan, quoted in her book* I Love You, Ronnie, *2000.*

The Law

"We cannot, as citizens, pick and choose the laws we will or will not obey."

—*Remarks made after Reagan ordered the firing of striking air-traffic controllers, September 3, 1981.*

Bigotry

"And let me add, in the party of Lincoln, there is no room for intolerance and not even a small corner for anti-Semitism or bigotry of any kind. Many people are welcome in our house, but not the bigots."

—*Acceptance speech given at the Republican National Convention, August 23, 1984.*

Apartheid

"America's view of apartheid is simple and straightforward: We believe it is wrong. We condemn it. And we are united in hoping for the day when apartheid will be no more."

—*Remarks made September 9, 1985.*

Protection

"As long as there are guns, the individual that wants a gun for a crime is going to have one and going to get it. The only person who's going to be penalized and have difficulty is the law-abiding citizen, who then cannot have [it] if he wants protection . . ."

—*White House interview, March 22, 1986.*

The Gipper

"Someday when things are tough, maybe you can ask the boys to go in there and win just one for the Gipper."

—*Perhaps Reagan's most famous movie lines spoken while playing George Gipp in the film* Knute Rockne, All American, *1940.*

Nuclear Weapons

"For decades, we and the Soviets have lived under the threat of mutual assured destruction; if either resorted to the use of nuclear weapons, the other could retaliate and destroy the one who had started it. Is there either logic or morality in believing that if one side threatens to kill tens of millions of our people, our only recourse is to threaten killing tens of millions of theirs? I have approved a research program to find, if we can, a security shield that would destroy nuclear missiles before they reach their target. It wouldn't kill people, it would destroy weapons. It wouldn't militarize space, it would help demilitarize the arsenals of Earth. It would render nuclear weapons obsolete."

—*Second Inaugural Address, January 21, 1985.*

Destiny

"You and I have a rendezvous with destiny. We will preserve for our children this, the last best hope of man on earth . . ."

—*Nationally televised speech for presidential candidate Barry Goldwater, October 27, 1964.*